CENTRAL AMERICA

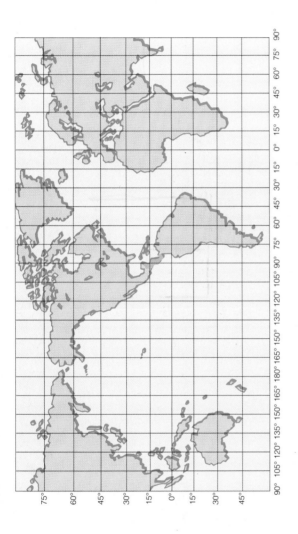

CENTRAL AMERICA

Country	Country area (square miles)	population 1997	capital	currency
BELIZE	8,865	228,000	Belmopan	Belize Dollar
COSTA RICA	19,730	3,500,000	San José	Colón
EL SALVADOR	8,124	5,950,000	San Salvador	Colón
GUATEMALA	42,046	11,250,000	Guatemala City	Quetzal
HONDURAS	43,280	6,300,000	Tegucigalpa	Lempira
NICARAGUA	50,200	4,544,000	Managua	Cordoba
PANAMA	29,760	2,629,000	Panama City	Balbao

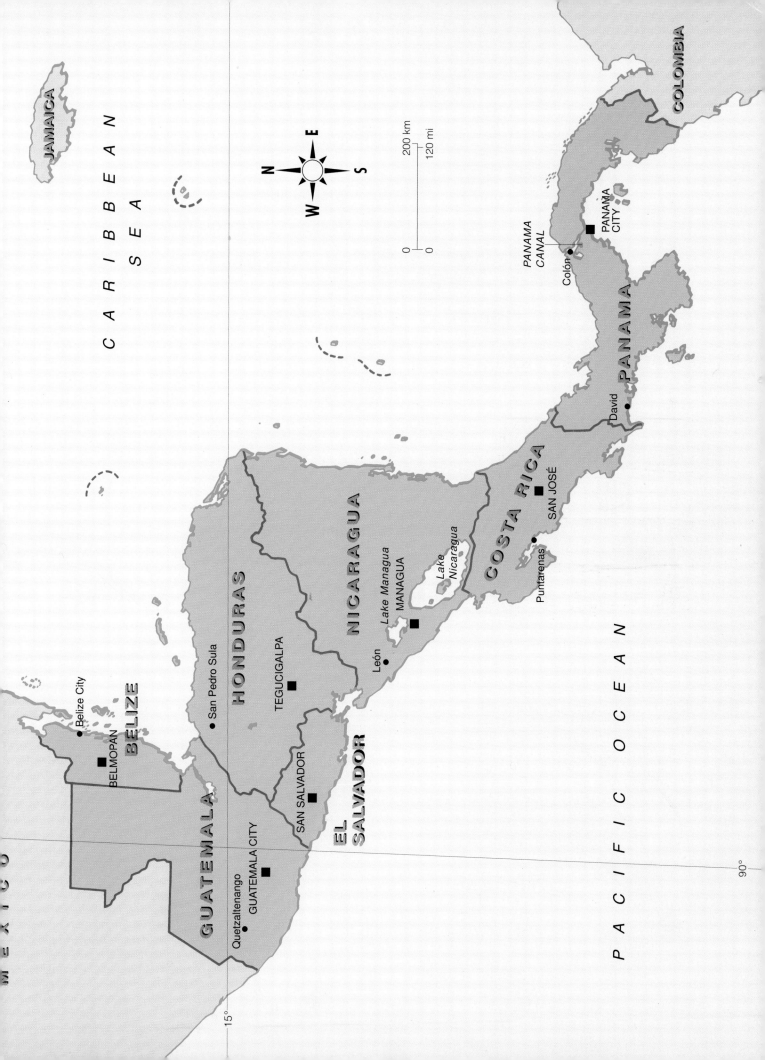

BELIZE

COSTA RICA

EL SALVADOR

GUATEMALA

HONDURAS

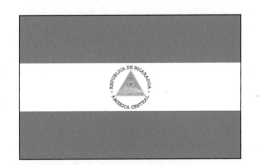

NICARAGUA

PANAMA

CENTRAL AMERICA

Edward Parker

RSVP
RAINTREE
Steck-Vaughn
PUBLISHE**R**S
A Steck-Vaughn Company

Austin, Texas

Published by Raintree Steck-Vaughn Publishers,
an imprint of Steck-Vaughn Company

Design and typesetting Roger Kohn Designs
Commissioning editor Rosie Nixon
Editor Merle Thompson
Picture research Gina Brown
Maps János Márffy

We are grateful to the following for permission
to reproduce photographs:
Front cover: Robert Harding, *above* (Christopher Rennie); Robert Harding, *below* (James Strachan); Sylvia Corday, page 22; Greg Evans, pages 25, 36 (Greg Balfour Evans); Eye Ubiquitous, page 41 (Tim Page); Robert Harding, page 11 *above* (Gavin Hellier); James Davis Travel, pages 9, 23, 28, 37 *below*, 45; Panos, pages 12 *above* (Paul Smith), 12/13 *below* (Sean Sprague), 32 (Tina Gue); Popperfoto, page 27; South American Pictures, pages 16 (Chris Sharp), 17 (Robert Francis), 19 (T. Morrison), 24 (Robert Francis), 30 (T. Morrison), 33 (Robert Francis), 34/35 (T. Morrison), 35 *above* (Chris Sharp), 37 *above* (Chris Sharp), 38/39 (P. Dixon), 44 (Robert Francis); Still Pictures, pages 11 *below* (Nigel Dickinson), 14 (Nigel Dickinson), 15 (Nigel Dickinson), 26 (Jorgen Schytte), 29 (Heine Pedersen), 31 (Julio Etchart), 39 above (Nigel Dickinson), 40 (Nigel Dickinson), 43 (Y. J. Rey-Millet); Tony Stone, pages 8/9 (Will & Den McIntyre), 10 (Hilarie Kavanagh), 20 (Margaret Gowan), 21 (Suzanne Murphy), 42 (Simeone Huber); Trip, page 18 (Robert Belbin).

The statistics given in this book are the most up-to-date available
at the time of going to press.

Printed in Hong Kong by Wing King Tong

Library of Congress Cataloging-in-Publication Data
Parker, Edward, 1961–
Central America / Edward Parker.
p.   cm. — (Country fact files)
Includes bibliographical references and index.
Summary: Introduces the landscape, climate, natural resources, people, daily life, government, and economy of the seven countries that make up Central America.
ISBN 0-8172-5406-4
1. Central America — Juvenile literature. [1. Central America.]
I. Title. II. Series.
F1428.2.P37   1999
972.8 — dc21   98-45554
CIP
AC

1 2 3 4 5 6 7 8 9 0 HK 02 01 00 99 98

C O N T E N T S

Words that are explained in the glossary are printed in
SMALL CAPITALS the first time they are mentioned in the text.

INTRODUCTION

Central America is made up of seven countries: Belize, Costa Rica, El Salvador, Honduras, Guatemala, Nicaragua, and Panama. Together they cover an area of 202,008 square miles (523,160 sq km)—twice the size of the state of Colorado or the United Kingdom. The total population of the region is about 35 million.

These Central American nations are well known for their scenic landscapes with, for example, active volcanoes, steamy TROPICAL forests, or attractive Caribbean coasts. Some of them are famous for the ruins of magnificent cities and temples built by the Mayan Indians. Many Indians, with their distinctive colorful cultures, still live in the region. Today, however, many members of Central American society are facing harsh realities, such as extreme poverty and violent crime.

Before the first Europeans arrived, the region was home to millions of Indians. The most famous of the civilizations that developed there was that of the Maya, which flourished between 1,000 and 2,000 years ago. The Mayan empire was very large and included most of Guatemala and Belize, western Honduras, and a large part of southern Mexico. The Maya built temples with towers over 200 feet (60 m) high and constructed magnificent cities, like Tikal, in Guatemala, which covers 6 square miles

CENTRAL AMERICA AT A GLANCE

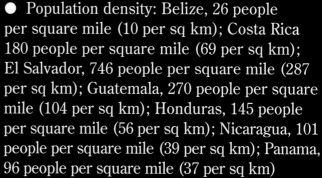

● Population density: Belize, 26 people per square mile (10 per sq km); Costa Rica 180 people per square mile (69 per sq km); El Salvador, 746 people per square mile (287 per sq km); Guatemala, 270 people per square mile (104 per sq km); Honduras, 145 people per square mile (56 per sq km); Nicaragua, 101 people per square mile (39 per sq km); Panama, 96 people per square mile (37 per sq km)

● Population largest cities (1992–1995): Guatemala City (Guatemala) 1,814,000; San Salvador (El Salvador) 1,522,000; San José (Costa Rica) 1,186,000; Managua (Nicaragua) 973,000; Tegucigalpa (Honduras) 739,000; Panama City (Panama) 452,000

● Highest mountain: Volcano Tajumulca (Guatemala), at 13,815 feet (4,211 m)

● Largest body of water: Lake Nicaragua, 100 miles (160 km) long with an area of 3,100 square miles (8,030 sq km)

● Major religion: Roman Catholicism

● Major resources: produce, shellfish, timber, iron, silver, copper, lead, tin, HYDROELECTRICITY, and GEOTHERMAL ENERGY

● Major products: Bananas, coffee, fruit, cotton, textiles, timber, and minerals

● Environmental problems: SOIL EROSION, DEFORESTATION, pollution

▲ A stone mask of the sun at Copán, in Honduras. These are the largest Mayan ruins in Central America. The city once covered an area of 15 square miles (39 sq km) and is famous for its three-dimensional stone carvings.

◀ An aerial view of Panama City, one of the wealthiest areas in Central America

(16 sq km). There were many other INDIGENOUS peoples living in the region, including the Lenca, Cuna, and Miskito.

In the 16th century, Europeans arrived in Central America, attracted by rumors of gold and other riches. Their superior weapons enabled them to conquer the indigenous peoples. As a result, the region fell almost entirely under the control of the Spanish for 300 years. During the 19th century, however, the countries of the region gained their independence.

THE LANDSCAPE

Due to their location on the narrow ISTHMUS between the landmasses of North and South America, the countries of Central America are particularly vulnerable to earthquakes and volcanic eruptions. The region displays a remarkable variety of landscapes. These include active volcanoes rising to 13,123 feet (4,000 m), tropical beaches, rain forests rich in wildlife, and cool, TEMPERATE highlands.

Central America extends 1,180 miles (1,900 km) from the Mexican border to Colombia, but it is only one-fourth the size of Mexico. It is bordered on the west by the Pacific Ocean and on the east by the Caribbean Sea and lies between the equator and the tropic of Cancer.

A chain of volcanoes that runs near the Pacific Ocean dominates the landscape. Inland lies a rugged upland landscape formed by ancient volcanic eruptions. This upland and the narrow Pacific coast is home to about three-fourths of the population.

The eastern coastal landscape was formed by a different geological process, during which the Earth's crust was compressed into parallel ridges and valleys. This landscape extends across northwestern Central America to the Caribbean coastline of Honduras. The ridges continue under the Caribbean Sea where the highest peaks re-emerge as the islands of the Greater Antilles.

One-third of the land in Central America lies above 3,280 feet (1,000 m). There are only small areas of low-lying land, and these are restricted to the northern part of

▼ *The landscape of Central America is dominated by the cones of volcanoes such as Poás, in Costa Rica.*

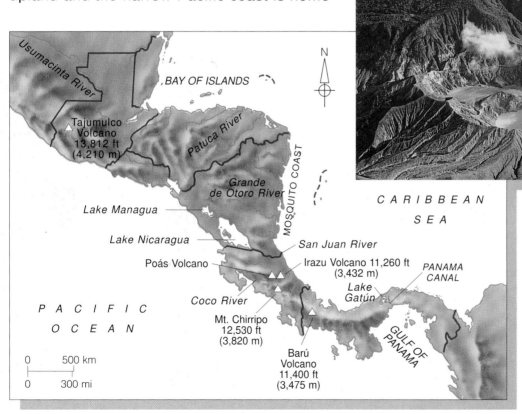

▶ *The typical landscape in the cool highlands of Guatemala consists of a patchwork of small fields on steep hillsides.*

◀ *Ambergris Caye is just one of several hundred small coral islands off the coast of Belize.*

Guatemala, the narrow coastal strips along the Pacific and Caribbean coastlines, and the lowlands that border Managua and Nicaragua lakes in Nicaragua.

There are a number of interesting geographical features in the region. In the extreme north, there is an area of undulating hills covered in rain forest, called El Petén. It is the largest remaining area of rain forest left in Central America. In the south is Darién, an area of Panama that consists of virtually uninhabited low, scrubby forest. Off the Caribbean coast of Belize, there are hundreds of small coral islands called cayes.

KEY FACTS

● The continents of North and South America were separated by a narrow strip of water until the end of the last ice age, 3 million years ago.

● Belize has the world's fifth longest barrier reef.

● More than 35,000 people have been killed by earthquakes in Guatemala and Nicaragua since 1970.

● The narrowest part of Central America is in Panama, where only 50 miles (80 km) of the Panama Canal separate the Atlantic from the Pacific Ocean.

● The region has more than 100 volcanoes, a number of which are still active.

◄ *The high levels of rainfall in the Sierra Mountains near Quiche in Guatemala enable the cool* MONTANE *rain forest to thrive.*

Central America is located in the Tropics, but it is the altitude and the season rather than the latitude that determine the local conditions. Since more than one-third of the land in the region is above 3,280 feet (1,000 m), the temperatures there are considerably cooler than the lowlands, and the climate is temperate. The climate of the lowlands and the coasts is tropical.

Central America lies in the NORTHERN HEMISPHERE, and similar to North America, the hottest months are from April to September. At this time temperatures can soar to well above 86°F (30°C) along the Caribbean coasts of countries like Belize, Honduras, and Nicaragua. The coolest months are October to March. During these months temperatures can fall to only a few degrees above freezing in the highlands.

Four of the seven capitals are situated in the temperate highlands, where nearly two-thirds of the population of Central America

live. Because of the seasonal rainfall and the fact that temperatures rarely fall below 41°F (5°C), the highlands are ideal for many types of agriculture.

The heaviest rains, for the most part,

occur between April and September. Generally they begin in the south of the region and move north. For example, in April, Darién, in the south of Panama, can experience heavy rain, while Guatemala can still be waiting for its first rains at the end of May.

There is a distinct difference in rainfall between the Pacific and Caribbean coasts. The Pacific rains fall mainly between the months of April and September, and the all-day rainstorms, called the temporales, occur in the months of June and September. In contrast, the Caribbean coast experiences heavy rainfall throughout the year. Between November and January, both the Pacific and Caribbean coasts are at risk from the devastating effects of hurricanes. From time to time, the weather in Central America can be affected by the EL NIÑO current in the Pacific Ocean.

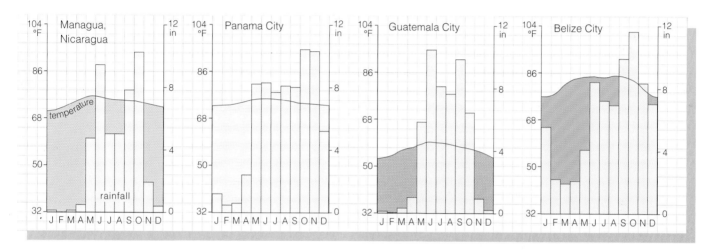

◀ *The coastal strip of El Salvador has a tropical climate and seasonal rains. These support the cultivation of crops such as coconuts, cotton, and citrus fruits.*

KEY FACTS

● The annual rainfall along the Caribbean coast ranges from 138 to 275 inches (350 to 700 cm) each year.
● In 1988 Hurricane Joan devastated the banana harvest in Nicaragua and damaged the new fishing fleet and shrimp farms along the Caribbean coast.
● In 1998 the warm El Niño current disrupted the seasonal rains, causing widespread drought that led to poor harvests and bushfires.

◀ *A* CHICLERO *climbs a tree in the rain forest in El Petén, Guatemala, to cut channels in the bark so that the chicle sap can be collected.*

AGRICULTURE

Central America is an area rich in natural resources. The most important of these is its fertile volcanic soils that are ideally suited to agriculture. It was the excellent conditions for growing food that enabled large civilizations like the Maya to flourish many centuries before the arrival of Europeans. The Maya and other Indians grew corn and beans as their staple crops, and millions of people still rely on these foodstuffs.

Today the region's main natural resource is still its agricultural land. Agriculture accounts for between half and three-quarters of the total value of exports from each country. The main products are corn, coffee, sorghum, bananas, and sugar.

In some countries, such as El Salvador, nearly all the land suitable for agriculture has been converted into farmland. Other countries, such as Honduras and Belize, have the opportunity to expand the amount of land used for agriculture.

FORESTRY

In several of the countries, such as Guatemala, Honduras, Panama, and Belize, there are large expanses of tropical forests. Honduras has 10.1 million acres (4.1 million ha) of forest cover and another 6.2 million acres (2.5 million ha) suitable for reforestation. However, forestry resources are disappearing rapidly. In the El Petén region of Guatemala, half the tropical forests have already been cut down. The wood of the mahogany tree is very valuable, and it is harvested in Panama, Belize, and Guatemala. Chicle, an ingredient of chewing gum, is tapped from rain forest trees in Belize and Guatemala.

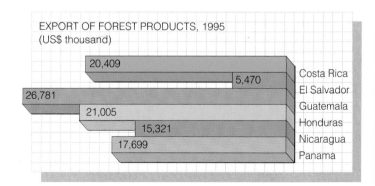

EXPORT OF FOREST PRODUCTS, 1995
(US$ thousand)

Costa Rica	20,409
El Salvador	5,470
Guatemala	26,781
Honduras	21,005
Nicaragua	15,321
Panama	17,699

MINERALS

Most countries in the region have only modest mineral reserves, with the exception of Honduras and Nicaragua. Honduras has considerable reserves of silver, gold, lead, zinc, iron, copper, and antimony; but only silver, lead, zinc, and small amounts of gold are mined commercially. Nicaragua has unexploited deposits of copper, lead, zinc, cadmium, bismuth, platinum, iron, magnesium, chrome, and titanium. Mining in Nicaragua, especially of gold, is likely to increase. Nicaragua also has the largest deposits of calcium carbonate (used in the manufacture of cement) in the region.

Among those countries with small mineral reserves, El Salvador has small deposits of gold, silver, mercury, lead, zinc, salt, and limestone. Costa Rica has deposits of manganese, mercury, and gold and is an exporter of sulfur and iron ore. Panama's main mineral resource is copper, and Guatemala's is nickel.

▼ *Countries such as Belize, Guatemala, and Honduras are cutting down large numbers of rain forest trees for timber to export to Europe, the U.S., and Japan.*

HYDROELECTRIC
ENERGY PRODUCTION,
1996 (gWh)

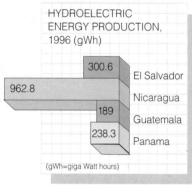

300.6   El Salvador

962.8

189   Nicaragua

Guatemala

238.3   Panama

(gWh=giga Watt hours)

▲ *Heat from deep in the earth is used to create the steam to power the turbines that produce electricity at this geothermal power plant.*

FOSSIL FUELS

All seven countries consume large quantities of oil and other fossil fuels, which until recently have been almost entirely imported. Exploration is under way in a number of countries, and significant oil deposits have been located in El Salvador and Guatemala. Guatemala produced

KEY FACTS

● Deposits of iron ore in Costa Rica are estimated to be 400 million tons. Deposits of sulfur are estimated to be 11 million tons.

● The geothermal power plant at Ahuachapan in El Salvador produces 60 megawatts of electricity, which is 10% of the total electricity consumed in the country.

● Honduras harvested 134 million cubic feet (3.8 million cubic meters) of timber in 1994.

● Corn, avocados, and chocolate all originated in Central America.

● Forests and woodlands account for 54% of the total area of Panama.

5,330,000 barrels of oil in 1996, 87 percent of which was exported. Honduras is the only country with large coal deposits.

ELECTRICITY
Central America has both heavy rainfall and a mountainous terrain, and these are the key requirements for hydroelectric power plants to work. They make a major contribution to the region's energy needs. For example, 80 percent of Honduras' electricity needs are met by hydroelectric power plants. A massive 3.34 million kilowatt-hours of electricity was produced in 1996 in El Salvador, and half of this came from just four hydroelectric power plants. Countries in the region can also tap into the geothermal energy of the land in order to produce electricity.

TOURISM
The magnificent landscape of towering volcanoes, dense rain forests, and tropical beaches are an important attraction for tourists. Since the political troubles that have plagued Central America in recent years have died down, there have been increasing numbers of tourists visiting the region. Guatemala alone had more than half a million tourist visitors in 1996.

▼ *Avocados are cultivated in many areas in Central America. This one is near Lake Atitlán, in Guatemala.*

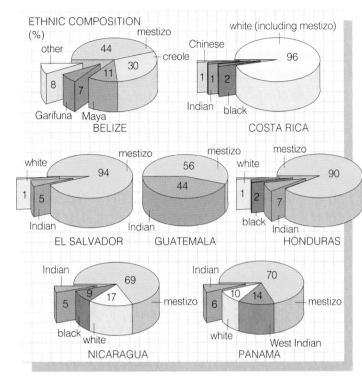

POPULATION

THE ORIGINS OF THE POPULATION

The ancestors of Central America's indigenous people are believed to have crossed the Bering Straits—between what is now Siberia and Alaska—and traveled south to reach Central America some time between 10,000 and 20,000 years ago. By the time the first Europeans arrived, the Central American Indian population, made up of many distinct cultures, was estimated to be about 5 million.

The arrival of the Spanish in the 16th

▼ *A farmer with oxen in Costa Rica. The farmers in this region are predominantly Caucasian.*

ETHNIC COMPOSITION (%)

BELIZE — other 8, Garifuna 7, Maya 11, mestizo 44, creole 30

COSTA RICA — white (including mestizo) 96, Chinese 1, Indian 1, black 2

EL SALVADOR — white 1, Indian 5, mestizo 94

GUATEMALA — mestizo 56, Indian 44

HONDURAS — white 1, black 2, Indian 7, mestizo 90

NICARAGUA — black 5, white 9, Indian 17, mestizo 69

PANAMA — white 6, Indian 10, West Indian 14, mestizo 70

One-third of the population of Costa Rica live in the bustling, cosmopolitan city of San José.

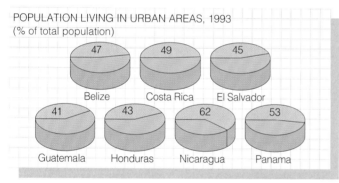

POPULATION LIVING IN URBAN AREAS, 1993
(% of total population)

47 Belize
49 Costa Rica
45 El Salvador
41 Guatemala
43 Honduras
62 Nicaragua
53 Panama

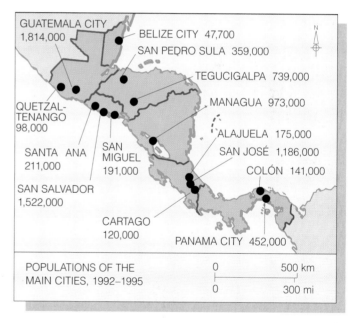

GUATEMALA CITY 1,814,000
BELIZE CITY 47,700
SAN PEDRO SULA 359,000
TEGUCIGALPA 739,000
MANAGUA 973,000
QUETZAL-TENANGO 98,000
ALAJUELA 175,000
SAN JOSÉ 1,186,000
SANTA ANA 211,000
SAN MIGUEL 191,000
COLÓN 141,000
SAN SALVADOR 1,522,000
CARTAGO 120,000
PANAMA CITY 452,000

POPULATIONS OF THE MAIN CITIES, 1992–1995

0   500 km
0   300 mi

century had a dramatic effect on these indigenous populations. The settlers brought diseases like smallpox with them, to which the local people had little resistance. The Spanish ruthlessly exploited the indigenous people, forcing many of them to work as laborers in mines and plantations. Millions of Indians died during the first century of contact with the Spanish.

During the colonial period, which lasted about 300 years, the European settlers established major cities, such as Tegucigalpa, Antigua, Managua, and San Salvador. Many European men married indigenous women, and their descendants are known as mestizos.

Some sections of the population are descended from the black slaves who were brought to work on coffee and sugar plantations. In 1850 many black slaves were moved to Central America from the

The Indians of the Guatemalan highlands wear colorful shawls called huípiles *that are distinctive within each village.*

islands in the Caribbean to help build the railroads and the Panama Canal. People of mixed black and Indian race are called mulattos.

THE POPULATION TODAY

Because of the history of the region, the population of Central America is very varied. Mestizos (sometimes also called Latinos) make up about half of the entire population, although they now account for as much as 94 percent of the population in El Salvador. There are also distinct indigenous groups, such as the Miskito of Honduras and Nicaragua, the Cuna of Panama, and the descendants of the Maya in Guatemala.

Throughout the region, Indians account for one-fifth of the population. Their numbers vary widely among the seven countries, as does their position in society. Most are concentrated in Guatemala, where between 60 and 70 percent of the population are AMERINDIANS of Mayan origin and speak one of the 22 distinct Mayan languages as their first language.

In Panama, there are five different indigenous peoples. These include the Guaymi Indians of West Panama, who are the most numerous, with 123,000 tribal members. In Panama, the Indians play an active role in government. The Cuna Indians, for example, have their own tribal land where they keep alive many of their traditions. They also have their own political representatives in Panama's Legislative Assembly. In Costa Rica, however, only 1 percent of the population belong to an indigenous group, and whites are, therefore, dominant. Blacks

▶ *A Cuna Indian woman selling local handicrafts on San Blas Island, Panama*

◀ *A Garifuna girl washes dishes in one of the many creeks on the Caribbean coast of Honduras.*

and mulattos are the most numerous in Panama and the Caribbean coastal plain. In Belize, Honduras, and Guatemala there is a distinct ethnic group called the Garifuna. They are descended from Carib Indians and black slaves, and they live in fishing villages along the coast.

MIGRATION

Before the arrival of the Spanish in the 16th century, the Indian peoples often migrated throughout the region. The Cuna of Panama, for example, originally came from Colombia. During the 20th century, however, the populations of all seven countries have tended to migrate from the countryside to the towns. Many rural areas of Central America lack schools and hospitals. In addition, the best employment opportunities are found in the main economic centers in major cities.

In the second half of this century, fierce fighting occurred in most of the countries of Central America, and this had the effect of speeding up the movement of people from the countryside to the towns. It also led to thousands of people becoming refugees in other countries. In 1992, 114,000 refugees

from other parts of the region were living in Costa Rica.

POPULATION GROWTH

During the 20th century, the populations of all seven countries have grown. The growth rate is now slowing in the wealthier countries such as Costa Rica (2.2 percent) and Panama (1.7 percent). However, the population of Honduras is growing at 3 percent per year. The percentage of the population under the age of 15 is much higher than countries such as Germany (16 percent), Japan (18 percent) or Canada (21 percent). People below the age of fifteen account for 44 percent of the population of Nicaragua and 33 percent of the population of Panama.

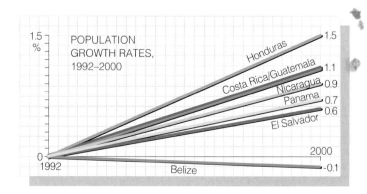

POPULATION GROWTH RATES, 1992–2000

1.5
%

Honduras — 1.5
Costa Rica/Guatemala — 1.1
Nicaragua — 0.9
Panama — 0.7
El Salvador — 0.6

0
1992   2000

Belize — -0.1

DAILY LIFE

FAMILY LIFE

Generally speaking, within Central America, families are still large and play an important part in everyday life. It is, therefore, common for parents, children, cousins, and also grandparents to live close by one another. However, this situation is changing because more people are leaving the area in which they grew up and heading to the large cities in order to find work.

In the cities, some families live in luxury, while others live in dreadful poverty. Home, for many people, is a modern apartment, and many are employed in professional occupations, such as banking, computer programming, and law. A small number of these people are extremely rich and can afford private planes and luxury yachts. This is in contrast to the millions of people who live in extreme poverty in the shanty-towns that surround most of the main cities.

KEY FACTS

- In 1996 there were an average of 22 murders a day in El Salvador, many attributed to the police.
- Panama has the smallest average family size of just 4.4 people.
- El Salvador has 43 universities.
- The national sport of Nicaragua is baseball.
- In 1990 the poorest 20% of Panama's population only received 3.7% of the national income.
- Panama has the highest per capita income in the region, yet 53.2% of the population in 1995 were living below the poverty line.

The bulk of the rural population, however, is made up of farmers and their families, who produce just enough food to feed themselves. To them the family is very important, and often children and relatives

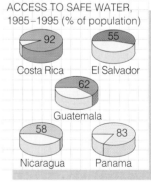

ACCESS TO SAFE WATER, 1985–1995 (% of population)

Costa Rica 92
El Salvador 55
Guatemala 62
Nicaragua 58
Panama 83

◀ *Many wealthy families in Costa Rica own a luxury house in the capital city and a cattle ranch in the countryside.*

all work together on the land. The family is also central to the culture of the indigenous people in the region, such as the Cuna and Quiche Maya. They maintain their traditional communities, and people of all ages play an active part in daily life.

RELIGION

The main religion of six of the seven countries in Central America is Roman Catholicism. Belize, until recently, has been predominantly Protestant, but the Spanish-speaking sector of the population is growing rapidly, and so is the number of Catholics.

Roman Catholics account for 85 percent of the population of Panama, and 95 percent of the population of Costa Rica. The black populations along the Caribbean coast tend to be Protestants.

▶ *Easter and Holy Week are among the most important religious festivals in the region. Here a young boy in a traditional purple robe is dispensing incense at an Easter celebration.*

MAJOR FESTIVALS AND HOLIDAYS

BELIZE

March/April	EASTER
April 21	QUEEN'S BIRTHDAY
May 1	LABOR DAY
September 10	SAINT GEORGE'S CAYE DAY

This was where a battle was fought in 1798 that gave Britain possession of the territory.

September 21	INDEPENDENCE DAY
November 19	GARIFUNA SETTLEMENT DAY

This reenacts the time in 1823 when the Garifuna were forced to flee after a failed rebellion in Honduras.

COSTA RICA

March 19	SAINT JOSEPH'S DAY
April 11	BATTLE OF RIVAS

This was when Costa Rica's national hero, Juan Santamaría, sacrificed his life fighting against a private army of invaders from the United States.

March/April	EASTER
May 1	LABOR DAY
July 25	GUANACASTE DAY

The state of Guanacaste remained independent until 1824, when it opted to join the rest of Costa Rica.

September 15	INDEPENDENCE DAY
November 1	ALL SAINTS' DAY

GUATEMALA

March/April	EASTER
May 1	LABOR DAY
September 15	INDEPENDENCE DAY
October 20	REVOLUTION DAY
November 1	ALL SAINTS' DAY

NICARAGUA

March/April	EASTER
May 1	LABOR DAY
July 19	REVOLUTION 1979 DAY
September 14	BATTLE OF SAN JACINTO
September 15	INDEPENDENCE DAY
November 1	ALL SAINTS' DAY

EDUCATION

Education for children between the ages of 6 and 14 is compulsory in all seven countries, but, in spite of this, school attendance is generally poor. In rural areas many children do not complete their education because they are needed to work either on the family farm or in low-paid employment to help support their families. People who live in urban areas and who can pay for private schools have the best educational opportunities.

Literacy levels have risen throughout the region over the last 20 years. For example, the percentage of adults who can read and write in Panama has improved from 81 to 90 percent between 1972 and 1990.

▶ *There are many religious days and festivals in Central America. One of these is the annual festival of Sololá, a small town in the hills above Lake Atitlán, in Guatemala. This takes place every August.*

PUPILS PER PRIMARY TEACHER, 1995

25	Belize
32	Costa Rica
44	El Salvador
34	Guatemala
38	Honduras
37	Nicaragua

◀ *Many rural schools in Central America have only the most basic equipment for the classrooms.*

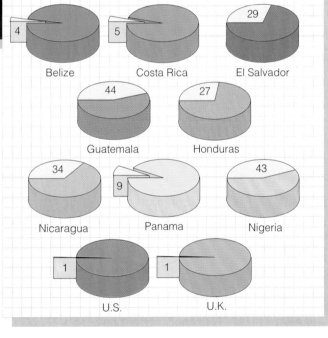

POPULATION UNABLE TO READ OR WRITE, 1995
(% of total population)

4 Belize	5 Costa Rica	29 El Salvador
44 Guatemala	27 Honduras	
34 Nicaragua	9 Panama	43 Nigeria
1 U.S.	1 U.K.	

However, literacy levels are still poor when compared to most other countries in the Northern Hemisphere.

SOCIAL PROBLEMS

The region has a number of major social problems, including poverty, poor health facilities, violent crime, and drug trafficking. Honduras, for example, is the poorest country in the Northern Hemisphere. People there had a life expectancy of only 68 in 1996. It also has the highest levels of diseases like malaria, AIDS, and tuberculosis of any Central American country. The rural populations of all the countries suffer from poor diets and limited health-care facilities.

Most of the Central American countries have recently suffered war, civil war, and high levels of violent crime. Although the 1990s have seen an improvement in human rights, countries like El Salvador are still violent places. In Guatemala, the violence and extreme poverty experienced over the last two decades by the poorest people have led to a huge increase in the numbers of homeless children who live on the streets.

Central America is a major route for the trafficking of drugs from South America to

North America. The demand for illegal drugs in North America has stimulated this multimillion-dollar trade. In recent years, for example, many Belizeans have become involved in the production of cannabis. The export of cannabis from Belize is now estimated to be worth about US$ 100 million a year.

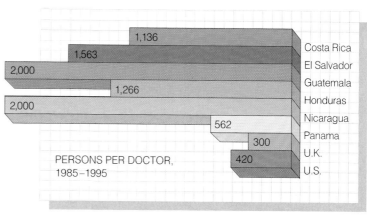

	PERSONS PER DOCTOR, 1985–1995
1,136	Costa Rica
1,563	El Salvador
2,000	Guatemala
1,266	Honduras
2,000	Nicaragua
562	Panama
300	U.K.
420	U.S.

LEISURE

As is true in most Roman Catholic countries, occasions such as christenings and first communion are considered important and are celebrated by the whole family. There are many religious festivals, most important of which are Christmas, Holy Week, and the Day of the Dead on November 2nd.

The most popular sports in Central America are soccer and volleyball. Both are taught in schools. However, these are not the only sports—Belizeans enjoy cricket, and in rural areas cockfighting and bull-fighting are still popular pastimes.

Music is an important part of life in all seven countries. The music in the north of the region is influenced by Mexico, but Guatemala has its own musical style. It is based around a large, wooden percussion instrument similar to the xylophone, called the marimba. Panama has a distinct musical tradition based on a combination of African and Colombian influences. Many indigenous peoples, such as the Chorotegas of Costa Rica, have kept their traditional musical heritage alive.

▶ *Costa Rica narrowly missed a place in the 1998 World Cup finals when they lost to Jamaica.*

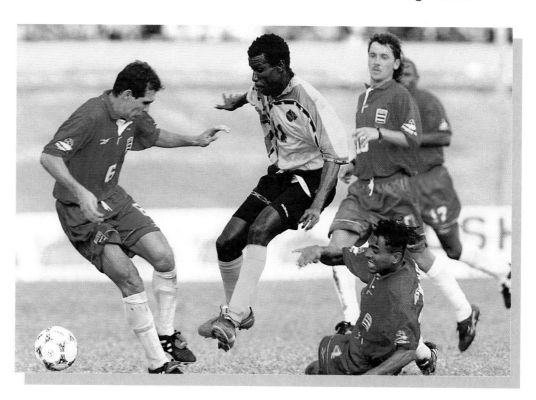

RULES AND LAWS

The political history of most of the Spanish-speaking countries within Central America has been a turbulent one since they gained independence from Spain during the 19th century. In recent years, the region has seen wars, civil uprisings, dictatorships, and terrorism. An exception to this is Costa Rica, where, after a revolution in 1948, a democratic constitution was put in place and the army replaced by a civil guard.

The recent political instability in Nicaragua is, however, typical of the region. There, in July 1979, a popular uprising overthrew the corrupt government of President Garcia Somoza. This ended 20 years of dictatorship, which had cost the lives of over 50,000 Nicaraguans. The opposition to the Somoza family was led by a political group called the Sandinistas, who were supported by the Soviet Union. They went on to win elections in 1985. The United States, however, provided military training and weapons for the CONTRAS, who opposed the newly elected government. The United States feared the expansion of Soviet influence in Central America. They also imposed a trade ban on Nicaragua. The conflict was finally

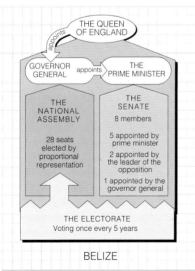

BELIZE

THE QUEEN OF ENGLAND
appoints

GOVERNOR GENERAL — *appoints* — THE PRIME MINISTER

THE NATIONAL ASSEMBLY

28 seats elected by proportional representation

THE SENATE

8 members

5 appointed by prime minister

2 appointed by the leader of the opposition

1 appointed by the governor general

THE ELECTORATE
Voting once every 5 years

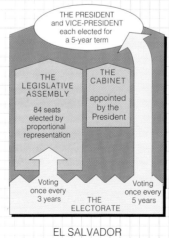

EL SALVADOR

THE PRESIDENT and VICE-PRESIDENT each elected for a 5-year term

THE LEGISLATIVE ASSEMBLY

84 seats elected by proportional representation

THE CABINET

appointed by the President

Voting once every 3 years

THE ELECTORATE

Voting once every 5 years

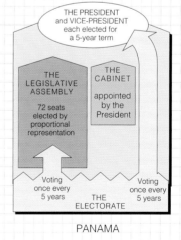

PANAMA

THE PRESIDENT and VICE-PRESIDENT each elected for a 5-year term

THE LEGISLATIVE ASSEMBLY

72 seats elected by proportional representation

THE CABINET

appointed by the President

Voting once every 5 years

THE ELECTORATE

Voting once every 5 years

◀ *A statue of Bartolomé de las Casas, who championed the rights of the indigenous people of Guatemala in 1533.*

resolved by negotiation in 1987, with the two sides attempting to work together. In 1990 a new president was elected, but the unrest has continued.

Some of the countries in Central America have the worst human rights records of any region in the world. In Guatemala, during the 1980s, an army officer named Rios Montt organized a campaign to crush guerrillas in the Guatemalan highlands.

KEY FACTS

● In 1980 a civil war broke out in El Salvador. When peace terms were agreed to in 1991, about 75,000 people had been killed, hundreds of thousands had been made homeless, and more than 50% of the workforce were unemployed.

● In 1989 U.S. troops invaded Panama to remove President Manuel Noriega, who was involved in organized drug trafficking. He was tried in the United States and found guilty in 1992.

● In 1992 Rigoberta Menchu, a Mayan Indian, won the Nobel Peace prize for her work in seeking peace between the Mayan people and the military government of Guatemala.

They were fighting for fair access to land and representation in government. In the first year alone, 15,000 Guatemalans were killed, hundreds of villages were burned, and 70,000 people were forced to take refuge in Mexico. Civil government was restored in 1986, but the military continued to abuse human rights. The situation has improved since 1996, when the government and the left-wing rebels signed a peace agreement.

During the 1990s, the countries of Central America have grown relatively more peaceful, and all now have democratic governments with elected assemblies.

◀ *Sandino Day in Managua, on which the life of Augusto Cesar Sandino is celebrated. He organized a rebellion against the U.S. occupation of Nicaragua in 1927. He was killed by national guardsmen in 1934.*

FOOD AND FARMING

Coffee plantations, like this one in Guatemala, are located on the fertile volcanic soil of the highlands in the region.

AGRICULTURAL LAND USE (%)

BELIZE
2
2
2
94

COSTA RICA
permanent crops
arable
pasture
8
6
7
45
34
forest and woodland
other

EL SALVADOR
27
8
29
30
6

GUATEMALA
4
12
12
40
32

HONDURAS
2
14
30
20
34

NICARAGUA
1
9
43
12
35

PANAMA
2
15
54
6
23

Agriculture is crucial to the economies of all seven countries. For example, in Honduras, agriculture employs 38 percent of the workforce and accounted for 21 percent of the GROSS DOMESTIC PRODUCT (GDP) in 1995. In Guatemala, 50 percent of the workforce are employed in agriculture. In El Salvador, agriculture employed 25 percent of the workforce in 1996 and accounted for 33 percent of exports and 70 percent of domestic food requirements.

At present, however, agriculture is declining in importance compared to other sectors of the economy. For example, in Costa Rica, 47 percent of the labor force was involved in agriculture in 1965, compared with 20.3 percent in 1995. Sugar, coffee, and bananas continue to be the most important crops in the region, but cattle raising is in decline. Fishing and fish farming, however, are growing.

In addition to commercial agriculture, millions of people in Central America are involved in subsistence farming, often on just a few acres of land. This means they can only produce enough food to provide for the requirements of the household or village. Poor farmers make up nearly three-quarters of all rural inhabitants in the region. Typically they produce corn, beans, and squash, which make up a large part of their diet. Throughout much of Central America, subsistence agriculture still follows the MILPA tradition. This involves the interplanting or mixing of crops in the same plot and is a similar system to that used by the Maya.

Depending on the climate, some of these farmers may also produce grains, fruits, vegetables, and meat products for the commercial market. They also provide the cheap seasonal labor required for the coffee, banana, and sugar harvests.

CASH CROPS

In general, coffee is the main crop in the volcanic uplands. The other four of the five main exports, sugar, bananas, cattle, and cotton, are grown in the lowland plains.

Coffee is the most important agricultural export for El Salvador, Guatemala, Honduras, and Nicaragua. In Belize, sugar and citrus fruits account for 40 percent of total agricultural production and 80 percent of exports. Bananas are the single most important agricultural product in both Costa Rica and Panama. Other crops that are grown on a large scale for export include cotton, cut flowers, tobacco, ornamental plants, and spices, such as cardamom.

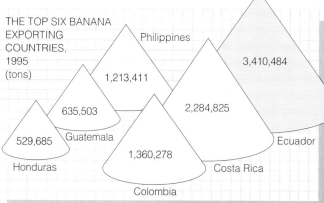

THE TOP SIX BANANA EXPORTING COUNTRIES, 1995 (tons)

Philippines 1,213,411
3,410,484
635,503
2,284,825
529,685 Guatemala
Ecuador
Honduras
1,360,278
Costa Rica
Colombia

▶ *Thousands of people are employed in the harvesting and processing of bananas, such as these Guaymi Indians in a packing plant in Panama.*

FOOD AND FARMING

◀ *This dish is typical of the food served in Nicaragua. It includes chicken, tortillas, salad, and gallo pinto, which consists of rice and beans.*

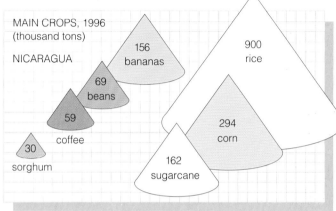

MAIN CROPS, 1996
(thousand tons)

NICARAGUA

- 156 bananas
- 900 rice
- 69 beans
- 59 coffee
- 294 corn
- 30 sorghum
- 162 sugarcane

to US$ 74.6 million in 1995. Three-quarters of Nicaragua's fish and shellfish production is exported to the United States.

All the countries in the region have realized that fishing could be a major contributor to their economies in the future, and many are investing in expanding their fishing fleets. Costa Rica already has a major fishing fleet and earned US$ 87.2 million from its catches of tuna, sardines, shrimp, and shark. However, if more and more fish are caught each year, overfishing could lead to a serious reduction of fish stocks in the future.

FISH

Shellfish are rapidly becoming one of the region's biggest exports. In Panama, shellfish have already become the country's second most valuable export, earning US$ 87.2 million in 1995. Similarly, Honduras earned US$ 178.2 million from shrimp and lobster exports in 1996, and the export of shellfish from Nicaragua rose

MAIN CROPS, 1996
(thousand tons)

HONDURAS

- 602 corn
- 3,388 sugarcane
- 147 coffee
- 70 sorghum
- 56 rice
- 51 beans
- 1,000 bananas

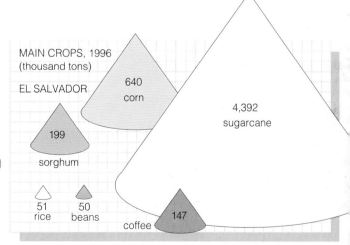

MAIN CROPS, 1996
(thousand tons)

EL SALVADOR

- 640 corn
- 4,392 sugarcane
- 199 sorghum
- 51 rice
- 50 beans
- 147 coffee

KEY FACTS

- Panama's chicken-meat industry has grown rapidly, and now there are more than 9 million chickens on farms throughout the country.
- The average size of a coffee plantation in Costa Rica is only 25 acres (10 ha), but most plantations are technically advanced and among the most efficient in the world.
- Agricultural products such as coffee, sugar, and bananas account for 75% of El Salvador's export earnings.
- Bananas accounted for 36% of total agricultural revenue in Panama in 1996.
- Honduras has a total land area of 28 million acres (11.2 million ha), yet only 4.4 million acres (1.8 million ha) are used for cultivated and permanent crops.
- Guatemala is the world's largest producer of cardamoms.
- Nicaragua earned US$ 671 million from agriculture in 1996.

LIVESTOCK

During the 1970s and 1980s, tens of thousands of acres of forest were cleared to create pasture for cattle ranching. During this era, the ranches provided low-priced beef for the large hamburger chains in the United States. Raising livestock remains an important part of the economy in Panama and Costa Rica. However, in the last decade, cattle ranching generally has declined in importance and, for example, only accounted for 7.5 percent of the GDP in Nicaragua in 1995.

▼ *The market in the Guatemalan town of Chichicastenango displays produce that is typical of the cool highlands of Guatemala.*

TRADE AND INDUSTRY

Industrialization only began in the region in the 1950s. Today most of the manufacturing economies are still dominated by food processing and beverage companies.

During the 1970s and 1980s, new industries, such as the manufacture of pharmaceuticals or the production of paper, were developed. Maquilladora industries were also created. In these, brand-named products, usually well known in Japan or the United States, are made under license at a much lower cost than is possible in either of those two countries. The economies of some Central American countries also have important service sectors, especially where American banking or computer centers are based.

The main trading partner of Central American countries has been the United States. However, there is a considerable amount of trade within Central America and also with Europe.

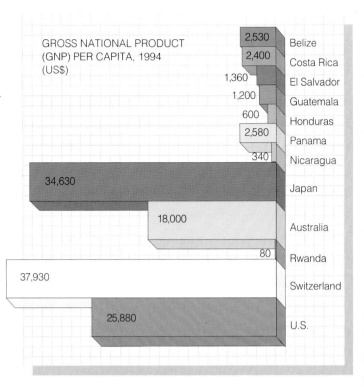

GROSS NATIONAL PRODUCT (GNP) PER CAPITA, 1994 (US$)

Country	GNP per capita (US$)
Belize	2,530
Costa Rica	2,400
El Salvador	1,360
Guatemala	1,200
Honduras	600
Panama	2,580
Nicaragua	340
Japan	34,630
Australia	18,000
Rwanda	80
Switzerland	37,930
U.S.	25,880

▼ *There are many small businesses in Nicaragua. This man is making furniture out of local wood.*

COSTA RICA

Costa Rica has a well-developed economy and is the most industrialized country in the region. Manufacturing and mining account for 20 percent of its GDP. However, in 1995 tourism became the single largest earner of foreign currency. The country's most important industry is food processing, and its main trading partner is the United States. Costa Rica also has a booming service sector with banking and computer operating centers.

EL SALVADOR

El Salvador's economy is still dependent on agriculture, and today new crops, such as cut flowers, soybeans, and ornamental plants, are also being grown. The most important manufacturing industries are food processing and petroleum products. Other key industries include textiles, pharmaceuticals, shoes, fertilizers, cosmetics, cement, and rubber goods. Maquilladora industries employ over 20,000 people.

▲ *Much of the agricultural work carried out on the coastal plain of El Salvador is highly mechanized, like on this pineapple plantation.*

BELIZE

Belize has the second highest per capita income in the region, but its economy is quite different from that of Panama. Belize's economy relies heavily upon a limited number of agricultural products and tourism. For example, agriculture accounts for 40 percent of the nation's GDP and 75 percent of its exports. Sugar and citrus fruits are its main exports, and the United States is its main trading partner. Tourism earns more than $100 million a year in foreign exchange.

KEY FACTS

● Tourism has become Costa Rica's main foreign currency earner. In 1995 Costa Rica earned US$ 661 million dollars from tourism, compared to US$ 620 million for bananas, and US$ 407 million from coffee.
● Nicaragua earned US$ 21 million from tourism in 1992. In 1996 the figure had risen to US$ 58.2 million.
● When newcomers are granted Belizean nationality, Belize earns $125,000 per family. Belize limits the number of incomers to 500 a year.
● Agricultural products, such as coffee, sugar, and bananas, account for 75% of El Salvador's export earnings.

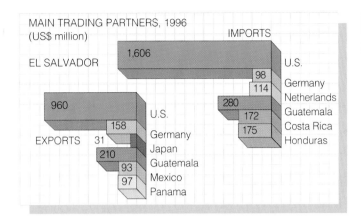

MAIN TRADING PARTNERS, 1996
(US$ million)

IMPORTS

EL SALVADOR

1,606

U.S.
98
Germany
114
Netherlands
280
Guatemala
172
Costa Rica
175
Honduras

960

U.S.
158
Germany
EXPORTS   31
Japan
210
Guatemala
93
Mexico
97
Panama

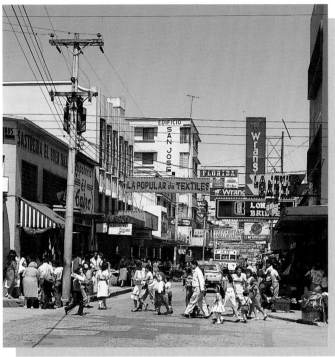

▲ *The streets in Guatemala City are often very busy. People shop there for low-priced items, such as locally made jeans or televisions.*

GUATEMALA

Although half the workforce of Guatemala are employed in agriculture, there are many manufacturing industries, such as food and beverage production, in urban locations. Other industries include the manufacture of tires, the refining of petroleum products, and a large clothing industry. Many products are brand-named maquilladora goods destined for the United States. The tourism industry is very important to Guatemala. It was badly affected by the conflicts between the army and terrorists in the 1980s, but it is now beginning to recover.

NICARAGUA

Nicaragua's economy was devastated in the 1980s by the Sandinista-Contra conflict and a subsequent trade EMBARGO imposed by the United States. Agriculture is the main sector of the economy, earning US$ 671 million in 1996, but manufacturing is developing fast. Industries include food processing, chemical plants, metal products, textiles, clothing, petroleum refining, beverages, and footwear. In 1996 Nicaragua exported computer equipment worth US$ 112 million.

HONDURAS

Honduras is one of the poorest countries in the Western Hemisphere and remains far less industrialized than its neighbors. However, foreign investment has been helping to expand the food processing sector and to set up industries such as textiles, papermaking, soft drinks, cement, beer, cooking oil, and rum. The country has the potential to expand its tourist and maquilladora industries, which have grown rapidly since 1982. However, bananas, coffee, and shrimp continue to account for more than half of all exports.

PANAMA

Panama has the highest per capita income in the region and is set for major economic growth. It has an excellent strategic geographical position and a number of major economic assets. These include the Colon Duty Free Zone, an international

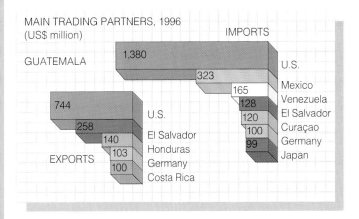

MAIN TRADING PARTNERS, 1996
(US$ million)

GUATEMALA

IMPORTS

1,380 — U.S.
323 — Mexico
165 — Venezuela
128 — El Salvador
120 — Curaçao
100 — Germany
99 — Japan

EXPORTS

744 — U.S.
258 — El Salvador
140 — Honduras
103 — Germany
100 — Costa Rica

banking sector, the Canal zone, the trans-isthmus oil pipeline, and the Panama Canal. In addition, it has large agricultural, industrial, and mining sectors. Today, although bananas and shellfish are still the two largest exports, services such as banking and tourism are booming.

▲ *The capitals Guatemala City and Panama City have modern housing, several international banks, and a stock exchange.*

▶ *The Mayan ruins of Copán in Honduras attract many thousands of visitors each year.*

TRANSPORTATION

The first modern means of transportation in Central America were railroads constructed in the 19th century to carry produce such as coffee and bananas to the ports for export. In the 1950s, as the economies of the countries of Central America began to grow, major improvements were made in the transportation system.

Today the railroads have declined in importance, and some countries, like Belize and Nicaragua, no longer have railroads at all. Most countries have developed a comprehensive network of roads to connect all areas of the country. The most important road is the Pan-American Highway, which extends from Guatemala almost to Panama's border with Colombia, connecting all the countries of Central America except Belize. Many of the roads in Central America are unpaved. Costa Rica, for example, has an extensive network of 22,080 miles (35,532 km) of roads, of which only 17 percent are paved.

Air travel has become increasingly important, and each country has at least one international airport and a network of national air routes. Air travel has been expanded to cope with the increasing numbers of tourists and also the export of some of the nontraditional exports, such as cut flowers and shellfish.

Along the Caribbean coast, travel by boat is often the only way to reach some areas, such as the swampy coasts of Honduras and Nicaragua. Also the bulk of exports and imports are handled by the

▲ **Guatemala City and many other large cities in Central America have serious traffic congestion and suffer problems with air pollution from vehicle exhausts.**

◀ **The Panama Canal was completed on August 15, 1914. Since then, it has been used by more than 800,000 ships.**

KEY FACTS

● The Pan-American Highway runs the length of Central America and ends at Yaviza in Panama. It is only possible to travel overland to South America on foot.
● Nicaragua sold the tracks of its unused railroads for scrap metal.
● The Garifuna community of Stan Creek in Belize has a population of 10,000 people, but it is only accessible by boat.
● In 1996 there were 333,990 cars in El Salvador.
● Air traffic in Costa Rica more than doubled between 1986 and 1994.
● At noon on December 31, 1999, Panama will take control of the Panama Canal from the United States.

LENGTH OF PAVED ROADS, 1992–1993 (miles)

Belize	Costa Rica	El Salvador	Guatemala
208	3,485	1,080	7,478

Honduras	Nicaragua	Panama	U.K.	U.S.
1,574	2,485	200	13,065	89,170

modern commercial ports on the Caribbean and Pacific coasts. Half of all Honduras' exports, for example, pass through Puerto Cortez, on the north coast.

The Panama Canal is one of the most important trade routes in the world. Today it takes a ship on average 24 hours to travel along the 50-mile (80-km) canal and its locks. Before the canal was built, ships crossing from the Pacific to the Atlantic would have to go around Cape Horn, at the southern tip of South America, adding several thousand miles to their journey.

THE ENVIRONMENT

Central America is facing many environmental challenges as its population grows and the economies in the region develop. The population is already over 35 million and has the second highest rate of growth in the world. To feed the many new mouths, more land will be needed to grow food, increasing the pressure to convert natural areas into farmland. Major environmental problems facing Central America are deforestation, air and water pollution, soil erosion, overfishing, and a reduction in BIODIVERSITY.

Central America is particularly rich in wildlife, because the isthmus links the two distinct continents of North and South

▲ *The rapid growth of cities has led to many environmental problems in the slum areas. Here children play near an open sewer in Guatemala City.*

America. As a result, Central America has a large number of different animal and plant species in relation to its size. For example, the region covers only 0.5 percent of the Earth's surface, yet it contains an estimated 8 percent of all the species on the planet. These species are found in a wide variety of habitats ranging from cloud forest to semidesert.

Today about one-third of the region's forests remain, but deforestation continues at an alarming rate—about 988,386 acres

KEY FACTS

● El Petén, the largest continuous area of rain forest in Central America, accounts for 33% of the land area of Guatemala. The population of the area has risen rapidly from just 15,000 in 1950 to over 350,000 in 1997.
● Central America has more than 800 species of birds and is situated on three of the four major migration routes between North and South America.
● One single tree on the island nature preserve of Barro Colorado was found to be home to 950 different species of beetles.
● Central America's natural forests are being cleared at the rate of 124 acres (50 ha) per hour.
● The coral reefs off the coast of Belize are the fifth largest in the world and attract thousands of tourists every year.
● The region's population is predicted to rise from 35 million to 66 million by 2030.
● Panama alone has more bird species than the United States and Canada combined.

(400,000 ha) per year. Typically, loggers create routes into the forests and cut down valuable trees. Landless people then move in along the roads created by the loggers and clear the remaining forests to grow subsistence crops. The land becomes exhausted within three to four years, and the farmers then move on, clearing new areas of forest.

Cattle ranching is the single largest cause of deforestation, accounting for the destruction of more than half of Central America's forests. In the 1960s and 1970s, large areas were cleared to provide pastures for the production of beef. After seven to ten years, the land became degraded, and the ranchers had to keep moving on to find new pastures.

In response to the environmental catastrophe of deforestation, all the countries of Central America are making efforts to protect their remaining natural habitats. Today there are 44 million acres (18 million ha) of protected areas in the region, and all countries have signed the Convention on Biological Diversity.

There are many problems facing the growing urban areas of Central America. Air pollution is a major problem in most of the large cities of the region. Costa Rica, for example, has over half a million vehicles, but there are few regulations on the exhaust emitted by each vehicle. The industrial areas also contribute to air pollution. Heavy industries, such as metal foundries, often release toxic pollutants such as arsenic into the atmosphere.

Water is also heavily polluted in many areas. Pollution in El Salvador is particularly bad, and 90 percent of all the rivers are contaminated by chemical waste. In Honduras, Lago de Yojoa, the country's largest source of freshwater, has become polluted with heavy metals from the mining industry.

Soil erosion is also a major problem. For example, in Panama 50 percent of the soils are poor, and 75 percent of the agricultural

◄ *Trucks carry away logs that have been illegally taken from forests in Darién, Panama. Although many areas of Central America are protected, illegal logging still occurs.*

land is located on steep hillsides, which encourages soil erosion. In El Salvador, over 66 percent of all farmland suffers from soil erosion. Soil erosion not only destroys the agricultural land, but also causes major rivers and hydroelectric power plants to collect silt. The Panama Canal is gradually filling with silt, because 70 percent of the forests along its banks have already been cut down, allowing the soil to wash away.

Coastal areas of the region are also under threat. The mangrove forests are rapidly disappearing to make way for new settlements, tourist resorts, and shrimp farms. Many commercial fish species breed in mangrove areas, and their disappearance, as well as overfishing, could spell disaster for the coastal fisheries in the next decade.

Other marine areas, such as the shallow waters off the coast of Nicaragua, are rich

▶ *Jaguars are present in all the countries of Central America and are the largest* CARNIVORES *in the region.*

◀ *The barrier reef of Belize is home to thousands of species of marine organisms. This is the blue hole on the Lighthouse Reef. It formed when the roof of an underground cave collapsed.*

Forest coverage in Panama

N

1947

1983

2000*

| 0 | 200 km |
| 0 | 120 mi |

* estimated

in rare species, such as sea turtles. Belize has one of the finest coral reefs in the world, but the uncontrolled dumping of sewage into the Caribbean Sea is causing the waters to deteriorate.

There are many positive initiatives currently under way to help protect the environment. At a government level, for example, Panama has given protected status to 17 percent of its land area. Many people are aware of the environmental problems facing all seven countries and are campaigning to reduce pollution and protect areas of special biological importance. Community action, environmental education, and the continuing traditional, sustainable land use in Indian areas are all helping to confront the environmental problems facing the people of Central America.

There are many problems that need to be addressed before the lives of ordinary people can begin to improve in Central America. Since the population of the region is likely to double in the next 30 years, there will be more pressure to convert natural forests and scrublands into land for agriculture. The forest loss in the region so far has already caused local climates to change and has increased the rate of soil erosion. Both of these changes will affect the ability of each country to produce sufficient food for itself.

To provide additional employment, the nations of Central America are pursuing a policy of expanding their industrial capacity. But this, too, can have negative effects on the population. For example, 90 percent of El Salvador's rivers are contaminated with chemicals, and this is causing health problems. However, many countries are promoting the expansion of service industries, such as tourism and banking,

▼ *Visitors at Poás National Park, in Costa Rica. Costa Rica is one of the countries interested in protecting wilderness areas and encouraging the development of the tourist industry to provide future employment.*

region are drug trafficking, large-scale destruction of natural forests, poverty and hunger, air and water pollution, and a rapidly growing population. In all Central American countries, the wealth of the nation is concentrated in the hands of a small percentage of the population. The region has some of the poorest countries in the Western Hemisphere and has been ravaged by wars and civil wars for the last half a century. The 1990s, however, have ushered in a period of relative peace, and all seven countries have returned to democratic governments. If peace can be maintained, there is a possibility that the countries of Central America can create a brighter future for themselves.

▲ *The Cuna Indians of Panama have a legal title to their traditional land and also have elected representatives to try to help safeguard their future.*

which cause fewer environmental problems.

All the countries in the region have improved their education and health services over the last 20 years. Moreover, life expectancy throughout the region is higher than it was a decade ago, and the number of people who can read and write is also increasing steadily. A healthier and better-educated population will contribute more to developing the economy, by filling skilled job vacancies and by putting increased energy into their work.

Some of the worst problems facing the

KEY FACTS

● The poorest 20% of Panama's population only receive 2% of the national income, while the wealthiest 5% receive 18%.
● Half the population of El Salvador does not have access to clean water.
● In 1994, 57.9% of the population of Tegucigalpa, the capital of Honduras, were living below the poverty line.
● Nicaragua is estimated to have 3.8 million ounces of unmined gold.
● The toll receipts from ships using the Panama Canal rose to US$ 463 million in 1995.
● Income from tourists visiting Costa Rica more than doubled from US$ 275 million in 1990 to US$ 661 million in 1995.

FURTHER INFORMATION

● EMBASSY OF BELIZE
2535 Massachusetts Avenue, NW
Washington, D.C. 20008

● EMBASSY OF COSTA RICA
2114 S Street, NW
Washington, D.C. 20008

● EMBASSY OF EL SALVADOR
2308 California Street, NW
Washington, D.C. 20008

● EMBASSY OF GUATEMALA
2220 R Street, NW
Washington, D.C. 20008

● EMBASSY OF HONDURAS
3007 Tilden Street, NW
Washington, D.C. 20008

● EMBASSY OF NICARAGUA
1627 New Hampshire Avenue, NW
Washington, D.C. 20009

● EMBASSY OF THE REPUBLIC OF PANAMA
2862 McGill Terrace, NW
Washington, D.C. 20008

BOOKS ABOUT THE REGION

Morrison, Marion. *Costa Rica.* Children's Press, 1998.

Sanders, Renfield. *El Salvador.* Chelsea House, 1997.

Targ, Harry R., and Marlene Targ Brill. *Honduras.* Children's Press, 1995.

GLOSSARY

AMERINDIANS
The Indians of the Americas.

BIODIVERSITY
Short for biological diversity, which means all the different plants and animals found in a particular area.

CARNIVORES
Mammals that eat mostly meat.

CHICLERO
A person that collects chicle from a rain forest.

CONTRAS
The rebel army that fought against the Sandinistas in Nicaragua at the end of the 1980s.

DEFORESTATION
The clearance of trees for use as fuel or timber, or so that the land can be used for farming.

EL NIÑO
A warm ocean current that, once every five to ten years, replaces the normally cold Pacific current off the coast of South America. This causes dramatic changes to the weather in Central America, often bringing droughts or floods.

EMBARGO
An order given by a government that forbids trade or commerce ships to enter or leave its ports.

GEOTHERMAL ENERGY
Heat obtained from geological activity deep in the earth that can be used to heat water to produce electricity.

GROSS DOMESTIC PRODUCT (GDP)
The total value of all the goods and services produced by a country, except for money earned from investments abroad.

HYDROELECTRICITY
Electricity produced when flowing water drives a generator.

INDIGENOUS
The original inhabitants of a particular region.

ISTHMUS
A narrow piece of land connecting two larger land areas.

MILPA
A farming system that was developed by the Maya. The various staple food crops are planted side-by-side on small sections of land.

MONTANE
Describes the climate or vegetation of mountain areas.

NORTHERN HEMISPHERE
The part of the world that lies north of the equator.

SOIL EROSION
A process in which soil is worn away by the action of the wind or water.

TEMPERATE
Describes a mild or moderate climate.

TROPICAL
Type of climate that is characterized by high temperatures and lots of rainfall.

INDEX

© Macdonald Young Books 1999